THE PUEBLO

by Mary D'Apice

Illustrated by Katherine Ace

ROURKE PUBLICATIONS, INC.

VERO BEACH, FLORIDA 32964

CONTENTS

Library of Congress Cataloging-in-Publication Data

D'Apice, Mary.
  The Pueblo / by Mary D'Apice.
    p. cm. —(Native American people)
  Includes index.
  Summary: A history of the Indian groups known collectively as Pueblos because of the sculpture-like villages in which they lived at the time the Spaniards arrived in North America.
    1. Pueblo Indians—History—Juvenile literature. 2. Pueblo Indians—Juvenile literature. [1. Pueblo Indians. 2. Indians of North America.] I. Title. II. Series.
  E99.P9D26 1990   973'.0497—dc20   89-77841
    ISBN 0-86625-385-8   AC

(Photo courtesy of Museum of New Mexico)

Camel Rock, New Mexico.

INTRODUCTION

Nestled in the mesas and deep canyons of the Southwest, the sculpture-like villages of the Pueblo Indians seem to rise out of the rock. When the Spanish arrived in America, they called the elaborate villages *pueblos*, which means "town." Indians who lived in these dwellings came to be known as Pueblos, but, in reality, all of them were not the same tribe. Some of the tribes that belong to the Pueblo group are the Hopi of Arizona; the Zunis, Acomas, and Lagunas in western New Mexico; and others on the banks of the Rio Grande River. Today there are about twenty working pueblos, most of which are concentrated around the Rio Grande in New Mexico.

Each group has a slightly different culture and language. Different tribes often do not understand each other when they speak in their native tongues. Despite their differences, Pueblo Indians have a common ancestry and share common spiritual beliefs.

Thousands of years ago, the forefathers of the Pueblos could be found in the "four-corners" region, the area where Arizona, Colorado, Utah and New Mexico meet. They were known by the neighboring Navajo as the *Anasazi*, which means "the ancient ones." The Anasazi were the first people to begin building homes in the rocky terrain of the Southwest.

The Pueblos have a very strong spiritual tradition that goes back to the time of the Anasazi. This religion is not reserved for special occasions, but is central to daily life. The Pueblos believe that they are caretakers of the earth and, therefore, must live in harmony with nature and respect the spirits that dwell in all living things.

From the time the Spanish leader, Coronado, arrived in the mid-16th century, Europeans and Americans have tried to persuade the Indians to give up their religion and their way of life. The story of the Pueblos is a story of a people struggling to maintain a delicate balance between pursuing a modern life and preserving the traditions of their ancestors.

The Pueblo

United States

Southwest Pueblos

Spanish

San Juan River

Grand Canyon HOPI

RIO GRANDE PUEBLOS

ZUNIS

ACOMAS

LAGUNAS

Colorado River

Rio Grande

Pecos River

NEW MEXICO

ARIZONA

U.S.

MEXICO

Philosophy/Religion

THE DIFFERENT groups of Native Americans who live in pueblos share a common creation myth that is the foundation of all their spiritual beliefs. The Pueblo Indians have built a philosophy around keeping life pure and living in harmony with nature.

The popular legend tells of how the Pueblos' ancestors emerged from an underworld through a lake or an underground passageway called *Sipapu*. They were led by the Great Spirit, the Creator, who showed them the path to their present homeland. The Great Spirit provided them with everything they needed to live on earth, and taught them that all living things — including corn, trees, animals, and people, as well as unseen natural forces — have a spirit. The Great Spirit appointed the Pueblos' ancestors as caretakers of the earth and gave them the responsibility of protecting it. "Life," said the Great Spirit, "is a delicate balance and only man has the power to upset the balance."

The Pueblos were expected to defend good over evil and to respect the generous earth. The Great Spirit warned that if the people disobeyed, terrible catastrophes would follow.

The Pueblos took this advice very seriously. They tried to live harmoniously, taking time to pay tribute to the spirit world through dances and sacred rites. Most ceremonies involved dramatizations of the mystical events that brought the Pueblos' ancestors to their homeland. Even today, the Pueblos are very strict about observing religious ceremonies. If a special dance is performed, they carefully oversee details, down to the preparation of the costumes.

Most of the sacred rituals take place in the pueblo *kiva*. The kiva is the most sacred building in the pueblo. Kivas are usually built underground, with a special hatchway representing the sacred opening, *Sipapu*, which legend says was the gateway to the world. The kiva houses an altar, sacred relics, and is often decorated with murals depicting mythological scenes.

The kiva has also functioned as a meeting room or clubhouse for the men, a place for them to relax and practice the male-dominated craft of weaving. Women and children have rarely been allowed into the kiva unless invited.

Kachinas—
The Masked Gods

Because Pueblo Indians were very aware of the spirit world around them, they believed it was necessary to call upon the influence of the Spirit World to live a healthy, happy life and to insure good crops. One important aspect of Pueblo religion centered around the *kachinas*. Kachinas were the supernatural beings, sometimes considered messengers of the gods, who visited the pueblos to bring good fortune. The kachinas first taught the Pueblos about hunting, farming, the arts, and rain dances. Though the Pueblos mastered other crafts on their own, they believed that the kachinas could help to bring them rain.

During a ceremony, which is still held today, kachinas emerge from the entrance of the kiva to recreate the journey out of *Sipapu*. When they arrive on the plaza, they dance and are cheerfully

things they used to create their clothes and mask for the dance

greeted by people of the pueblo. These ritual beings are decorated with body paint, tree branches, animal horns, and feathers to represent animals and ancestral spirits. (Even children watching the dance understand the importance of the dancers.)

As a child grows up, he or she is given dolls that represent some of the 300 different kachinas. These dolls are not toys, but are sacred elements of the religion. When a boy turns thirteen, he is invited to the kiva where the identity of the mysterious kachinas is revealed to him. Girls are not brought to the kiva, but they also are told the secret: It is their older brothers, fathers, uncles, and men of the community who perform the dances. The elders also explain, however, that when the men impersonate the kachinas in this way, the spirits of the kachinas enter their bodies. Ceremonies like this remind the people of the village that the spirit world is always in their midst.

Pueblo Bonito, Chaco Canyon, New Mexico.

Ancient History

Ancestors of the Pueblo tribes have lived in the Southwest for at least 12,000 years. Anthropologists believe that they were originally a nomadic tribe that survived by hunting wild animals and eating nuts and berries. Between the years 400 and 700, when they learned to grow corn, they finally settled in one place. In order to live beside the fields, they started to build homes in the caves and cliffs of the rocky region. These groups became collectively known as the Anasazi. Anthropologists also call them "The Basket Makers" because of the beautiful woven containers, belts, and sandals they created.

The Anasazi are also recognized as the original builders of the villages that rise up majestically from the rocky terrain. Their architectural tradition was firmly established by about 700, and the Anasazi gave way to the Pueblo culture. It can be said that the Pueblos were the first apartment builders. Pueblo Bonita, dating from about 950, remained the largest apartment complex ever built until a larger one was constructed in New York City around 1882.

Peak History

The Pueblo people flourished between 1050 and 1300. During this time, they established their main centers — Mesa Verde, Chaco Canyon, and Kayenta in the "four-corners" region. Chaco Canyon, located near the basin of the San Juan River, is the oldest city. It had main roads about thirty feet wide that led to neighboring villages.

If people are to appreciate the endurance and influence of the Pueblo tribes, it's important to picture their environment. The Southwest area of the U.S. has a semi-arid or desert climate. The terrain is rocky, with jagged cliffs or flat-topped formations called *mesas*. "Mesa" is the Spanish word for "table." It's difficult to believe that the Pueblos could grow crops in the parched mesa soil that often consisted of clay. In the Southwest, furthermore, droughts were a constant threat to survival, while in summer, storms could damage the harvest. Rain would come down so hard that crops often were washed away.

Despite a rough climate, Pueblo culture flourished. The Pueblos became very skillful craftsmen and farmers. They also made beautiful pottery, being best known for the style in which black designs are painted on a bright, white background. As their civilization grew, the Pueblo Indians developed newer and better ways to build their villages. They perfected their craft of stoneworking, which distinguished their culture from all others. Then, houses grew bigger and sometimes stretched thirty floors toward the clear, desert sky.

Suddenly, between 1276 and 1299, settlements started to fade away. Great villages like Chaco Canyon and Mesa Verde were abandoned. The Indians probably relocated with other tribes or settled elsewhere on their own. Judging from tree rings dating to that time, anthropologists estimate that a twenty-three-year-long drought must have forced the Pueblos to move.

In 1450, there was another series of migrations. Once again, entire towns were emptied. By 1540, when the Spanish arrived, most of the towns were abandoned except for a few near the Rio Grande Valley, and in Acoma, Zuni, and Hopi territories.

The Spanish Arrive

The Pueblos were first introduced to Europeans when the Spanish explorer, Francisco de Coronado, arrived in 1540. The 292 soldiers, Christianized Mexicans, and Franciscan friars who followed Coronado were the first of many foreign invaders who badly mistreated the Indians and challenged their age-old beliefs and traditions.

Coronado came to America in search of riches and mythical cities made of

gold. The Indians knew nothing about these riches and they probably wouldn't have had much use for such a soft, yellow metal even if they had known about it. Disappointed, Coronado returned to Spain without his treasure. Still he managed to make quite an impression on the Pueblos before he left their country.

Coronado was an uninvited guest in the Southwest, but he behaved as if he owned the land and its people. Wherever the invaders went, they demanded that the Indians pledge loyalty to Spain. The Spanish also tried to persuade the Indians to worship their Christian God. They took clothing off the Indians' backs and seized the precious foods the Pueblos had worked so hard to grow and preserve. In some cases, they burned villages, mistreated the inhabitants, and even sold them into slavery. Years later, Coronado was put on trial for his mistreatment of the Indians, he was never convicted. His treatment of the Pueblos colored Native American feelings about white men from then on.

(Photo courtesy of Museum of New Mexico)

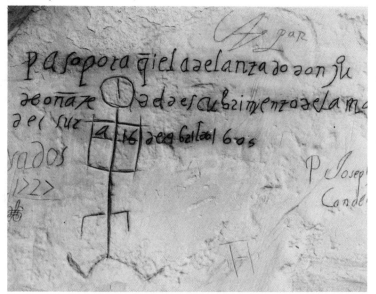

"Passed by here the adelantado Juan de Oñate to the discovery of the sea of the south on the 16th April the year 1605." This message was found on Inscription Rock, El Morro National Monument, New Mexico.

Colonizing New Mexico

For the next forty years, the Pueblos were free from Spanish invasion, but in 1580, small expeditions began entering the Pueblo region. Still, the Spaniards made little impact on the Pueblo tribes. The Pueblos remained virtually undisturbed until Don Juan de Oñate, sent by the King of Spain, burst into their settlements. A new generation of Spanish explorers had arrived, looking for the same treasures that had been sought by those who had come before.

Juan de Oñate made his conquest of Pueblo lands "official" in 1598. Spain granted him permission to colonize the Pueblo country called New Mexico and to convert all the inhabitants to Christianity. Oñate decreed that all the lands, the Pueblo villages, and the Native Americans themselves belonged to the Spanish Crown.

First, Oñate tried to establish the

Acoma Pueblo Mission.

*Dining room, U.S. Indian School,
Albuquerque, New Mexico, May 1881.*

Pueblos' allegiance by diplomacy. He held two major conferences with the representatives of the Rio Grande Pueblos. Speaking through interpreters, the Indians promised to be loyal to the King of Spain. Then the Father President of the friars convinced the Indians that they'd be much better off if they accepted the white man's God.

The Indian spiritual leaders were confused. Some of them believed this conversion would be a threat to their way of life. Others argued that they could accept an alternative view without threatening old beliefs. In the end, they agreed to let the friars visit the villages and instruct them in this new religion.

Soon Franciscan friars poured into the pueblos. They erected missions, using Indian laborers. Traditional Indian leaders fought hard to counteract the white man's teachings, but many Indians were curious about the new religion. Others were impressed by the power the Chris-

tian God seemed to have bestowed on the Spanish. By 1608, the missionaries had baptized 7,000 Pueblo Indians, and built missions in fifty towns.

The missionary friars, along with the soldiers, ruled tyrannically over the Pueblos. Though they were supposedly religious men, the friars were often cruel to Pueblo people who still observed their own rituals. The friars destroyed religious articles and even tortured the Indians. Even so, the Indians managed to hold on to their traditions. Kivas stood in the shadow of the missions; and Christian crosses were often decorated with feathers. In truth, the Pueblos' conversion to Christianity was only skin-deep.

Though the pueblo villages resisted change in spiritual matters, they welcomed changes in daily routines and material things. Soon Pueblo Indians used metal needles instead of bone needles. They learned Spanish crafts, grew Spanish crops, and raised livestock.

Isleta Pueblo Mission.

Spanish Tyranny

The Spanish were determined to establish a great empire over most of the continent and they were not going to let the Indians get in the way. Instead, they planned to build an empire on the backs of the Pueblo Indians — and they did. The Spanish disrupted the social and economic life of the Pueblos, as well as their spiritual life.

In a short time, Oñate conquered the peaceful tribes and set up a government much like the feudal societies of Europe. In a feudal system, peasants, or serfs, work in the fields for wealthy landowners. Essentially, the Indians were treated like feudal serfs.

A Spanish official was put in charge of each pueblo. He made sure that the Pueblos paid tribute to the Spanish colony in corn, handwoven cloth, and labor. Some of the artistic cloth products and wood decorations were exported and sold in Europe, making a profit for the Spanish colonists. Oñate decreed that the Indians pay an agricultural tax called *la encomienda*. A tenth of the income from the tax went to the Catholic Church and some of the rest of the money went to various government officials who worked in the capital of Santa Fe, New Mexico.

In most cases, the Pueblos did not fight back. Rebellions were unsuccessful because bows and arrows were no match for guns. Some of the Indians seemed to be in awe of the power of the white men. They even looked to the Spaniards for protection from the wandering tribes of the plains, who often raided the pueblos for food. The Apache were among the fiercest raiders. Still they were no match for the Spaniards' fire power. Some of the Pueblos were relieved to have the Spaniards' protection.

The Road to Revolt

It wasn't long before the Pueblos grew resentful of the unfair treatment they received. They were tired of working to build the Spanish empire, and they were tired of being punished for practicing their sacred rites. It was a time of great hardship for the Pueblo Indians. Small pox, a disease that originated with European settlers, wiped out 5,000 Pueblos in a single year. Crops dried up and people were forced to eat leather dusted in cornmeal. Nomadic warriors of the plains descended on the pueblos with increasing frequency.

Indian religious leaders feared that the Indians were suffering because their own gods were angry at them for worshiping the Christian God. Natural disasters and other problems seemed to be proving them right.

To make matters worse, the traditional leaders of the tribes were humiliated and tortured by the Spaniards. They were publicly whipped and jailed for witchcraft. Some were sentenced to slavery. The rest of the tribe was paralyzed without its leaders. How could the tribe conduct the sacred rites without its leaders? The Pueblos decided to fight back.

The tribes organized. Sixteen thousand Indians went to Santa Fe to demand that their religious leaders be set free. They surrounded the Governor's Palace and threatened to kill every Spaniard if the Indian leaders were not freed before sundown. The 2,500 Spaniards, obviously outnumbered, were forced to release the Pueblo prisoners.

Chief Popé Stirs Up a Revolt

Scattered widely across the Southwest region, the Pueblos never had much reason for unity. When the Spanish arrived, however, the Pueblos had a common enemy. Popé, a chief of the Tewa Pueblo, wanted to establish a Pueblo nation. For a long time, he had fought the influence and oppression of the Spaniards, struggling for both economic and religious freedom. The episode at Santa Fe seemed to prove that the Indians could stand up to the Spanish and be successful in a large-scale revolt.

Chief Popé was a powerful figure. Many Indians believed he had direct connections to the Spirit World. In the years leading up to the great revolt of 1680, Popé traveled to different pueblos in the hope of winning their support. From the Rio Grande Pueblos to the Zunis and Hopis in the west, Popé stirred up a following that would rise up and descend on Santa Fe. Like a violent whirlwind, the united tribes would tear down the seat of the Spanish empire.

Not everyone agreed with Popé. A few Indians were loyal to the Spanish and wanted Spanish soldiers around to protect them from raiding nomadic tribes. Popé fought the resistance, sometimes killing Pueblos disloyal to him.

After years of planning, the Pueblos were ready to fight. On August 10, 1680, the Indians rode across the desert and surrounded Santa Fe. The Spanish were stunned, never imagining that their powerful empire would be challenged. The Pueblos demolished the churches and took away the cattle and sheep belonging to the mission. In pueblos across the region, Christian relics were smashed and churches burned. The revolt lasted for eleven long days. In the end, 400 Spanish soldiers and missionaries were killed. The Spanish invaders were driven out. For a time, the eighty-two years of Spanish occupation in New Mexico were brought to an end.

(Photo courtesy of State Records and Archives, Santa Fe, New Mexico)

A Hopi house altar with ears of corn and a kachina would have been used to communicate with the Spirit World. The Hopi believed that some people, like Chief Popé, had a direct connection to the Spirit World.

The Spanish Return

When the rebellion ended, Chief Popé declared himself the new leader. He wanted to erase all traces of Spanish influence, including Christianity. Indians who had been baptized were purified with yucca suds. Those with Christian names gave them up, and all churches and Christian relics were destroyed.

Popé also demanded that the Indians cease planting Spanish crops such as alfalfa and wheat. He demanded that the Indians chop down the fruit trees the Spanish had planted, and he wanted the Indians to stop practicing Spanish trades such as blacksmithing. He called for the Pueblo to free all the animals the Spanish had brought, even the horses.

Many people thought Popé was too extreme. They didn't want to get rid of the things that made life easier. In addition, it seemed that Popé had learned some bad habits from the Spanish. He established himself in the Governor's Palace and at once began a tyranny of his own. Popé demanded tribute from the Pueblos and wanted people to bow down to him. Because of Popé's oppressive measures and disorganized rule, the fragile Pueblo union soon began to disintegrate. Bitter to his death, Popé never saw a strong and organized Pueblo nation.

The twelve years that followed the revolt were difficult. Nomadic tribes sacked the villages as before, but now the Spanish weren't there to provide defense. It was inevitable that some Pueblos missed the leadership and protection that the Spanish had offered. A few Pueblo families sought out Spaniards in El Paso and, after making peace, lived among them. Others fled to neighboring regions and lived with friendly Apache or Navajo tribes. Eventually, Spanish troops slowly began to trickle back into the pueblos. Stopping at each village, they offered to pardon the Indians who promised to be loyal. Those Indians who resisted were often burned out of their homes.

By the late 1680s, it was evident that the Spaniards were coming back to stay. In 1692, Don Diego De Vargas began his campaign to reconquer New Mexico for Spain. De Vargas used shrewd tactics. He tried to weaken the structure of the Pueblo alliance by turning villages against each other. Pueblos who were loyal to Spain attacked the rebel villages.

Peace was later established between the Pueblos and the Spaniards, but it was strained. The Spaniards feared another violent uprising, and the Pueblos were suspicious of the Spaniards. To soften relations, the Spanish agreed to be a little less harsh and to end the encomienda tax system.

The friars came back and resumed their old habits of religious oppression. This caused rebellions among Indians of the Taos Pueblos in 1694 and 1696. The Spaniards easily crushed the uprising, but, in the following years, the friars gave the Indians a bit more freedom to worship as they chose.

Gradually, the Indians stopped trying

Don Diego de Vargas Zapata y Lujan.

to fight back. Although more Indians were converted to Christianity, they continued to hold on to their ancestral beliefs. Those who drifted too far from tribal customs were forced to leave the pueblos or chose to move on their own. The ones who stayed in the pueblos were very committed to the ways of their ancestors.

19

Decline of the Spanish Empire

Toward the end of the 17th century, the missions and secular government paid less attention to the Pueblos. The decline of Spain's power in New Mexico came about because the Spaniards were forced to concentrate their energies elsewhere. Their energies had to be spent on confronting Plains Indians and threats from the French in the Mississippi valley. Without Spanish oppression, the Pueblos had the opportunity to return to the spiritual freedom they had enjoyed before the white man came.

In the early part of the 19th century, the Spanish Empire began to dissolve. In 1821, Mexico won its independence from Spain and became the new "owner" of Pueblo territory. Fortunately for the Indians, the Mexicans were worried mostly about holding on to Texas and keeping it from being absorbed by the United States. The Pueblos were left in peace. In 1847, a few Pueblo tribes joined forces with the Mexicans to fight the Americans. If they had to pick sides, the Indians were more comfortable with a familiar enemy than an unfamiliar one. The following year, the Treaty of Guadalupe Hidalgo ended the Mexican War, and the lands of the Pueblos officially became part of the United States.

In the beginning, the Americans treated the Pueblos better than they treated most other tribes. Because of the strong Spanish influence on the Pueblos, the American government viewed them as being unusually "civilized." The Indians were given land grants and offered American citizenship. The Americans also won over the Pueblos with the attacks they waged on the warring Apache and Navajo. By the 1880s, raids against Pueblo villages stopped entirely.

With the Spanish gone, the Pueblos had a chance to strengthen their religion. Even so, religious freedom did not last long. A new group of Christians arrived, this time Protestant, and including Baptists and Presbyterians. They were eager to convert the Indians to their beliefs.

The American government was very serious about assimilating the Indians into the mainstream of American life. Assimilation is the process in which an ethnic group gives up, or is forced to give up, its cultural identity until it becomes like the rest of the population. Some old Pueblos living today remember being shipped off to white-run boarding schools when they were children. They were often sent as far away as Pennsylvania and forced to stay at school for years at a time. The students faced cruel treatment if they dared to speak their own language or observe their sacred rites. The Federal Government wanted to keep the new generations of Pueblos from preserving their tribal customs and beliefs.

White Christian Americans became a threat to the Indian spiritual system. These Americans were opposed to the emphasis that the Pueblos put on spirituality, accusing the Indians of "un-American" practices. The Indian Religious Crime Code gave federal agents the authority to end an Indian town's religious freedom. Eventually the Indians were forced to practice their religion in secret.

Daily Life

Pueblo Indians have always believed in the importance of community living. Villages could not support many more than 500 people because water was always in short supply, but everybody shared everything they had. No one had more food or clothing than the next person.

The Pueblos were mostly vegetarians but they ate meat when it was available. Rabbit, gopher, and squirrel were popular, as well as larger game such as deer, antelope, and mountain lions. When a Pueblo killed an animal, he tried to make use of the whole animal and not just the meat. The bones were made into tools or ceremonial rattles, and the skins were stretched to make drums. Most of the year, however, the Pueblos survived on dried fruits and vegetables.

Though the growing season in the Southwest is short and dry, the Pueblos were relatively successful at vegetable gardening. Corn was the main crop, accounting for eighty percent of their diet. No wonder Pueblos had forty ways to cook corn! The Indians raised a special variety of corn that was particularly hardy. The corn had long roots and tough leaves that could stand up to the harsh, dry desert wind.

The production of corn was a major focus of community living. The lives of the Pueblos revolved around a cyclical pattern of community prayers, ceremonial games, and dances to insure a plentiful harvest. Each pueblo had an official sun-watcher who would let the community know when to plant seeds and harvest the crops.

Rain seldom fell on the pueblo, but when it did, it came down hard. Summer storms caused as much damage to crops as any drought did. Plots of land had to be chosen carefully, with both weather extremes kept in mind. The Pueblos learned to take advantage of what little rain and snow there was. To get water, they sometimes would go to the top of a snowy hill and roll a giant snowball down to the village, where it would melt. They also had a system of irrigation learned from neighboring tribes. The water flow was controlled and guided by mats made of woven fiber.

Pueblo families shared the fields in which they grew major crops such as corn and squash. Other vegetables, such as peppers, onions, chillies, and tobacco, were raised by individual families. Men were responsible for raising crops, and women were responsible for preserving them. The storing of corn was probably the most important and time-consuming task. The corn would be braided by the husks and then hung out to dry. The women would grind it in special troughs using three different types of stones, each coarser than the next. The corn would then be stored in special chambers built to keep out hungry animals. In case of a drought the next season, enough food had to be stored to last a year or two.

Corn dance. San Ildefonso Pueblos.

Gila Cliff Pueblo, New Mexico, 1932.

Building the Pueblos

As their name suggests, the Pueblo Indians are famous for their unique and beautiful architecture. During their early history, the Indians slept in the natural caves and cliffs of the region. As time went on, they began to build homes out of sandstone and adobe, the natural clay of the region.

The pueblos were built on mesas, on cliffs, and in canyons. Buildings were designed to meet the practical and spiritual needs of the village. Most of the time, pueblos were not planned. The villages were usually structured around a kiva which was the focus of daily life and of the pueblo itself. Homes gradually grew up around the kiva. The houses were owned by the women of the tribe. After marriage, a husband lived in his wife's home.

From time to time in the Pueblo community, everyone took part in house building. People were paid with food. Because it was expensive to feed people, as few helpers as possible were invited to participate. Everyone in the tribe made his or her own personal set of tools out of hard stones or bone. Tasks were divided between men and women. In most cases, men were the masons, the ones who built the main structure, and the women were plasterers.

Most often, homes were made from stone and clay or adobe, then plastered. Logs from long trees were used to support the roof. In the desert regions, trees were difficult to find and almost impossible to carry, so the one-room houses tended to be only as long as the most manageable trees. Generally a family lived in a room that was no larger than 12 x 20 feet.

The outer walls were built first. Then a layer of poles was placed on top. Next, willow branches were piled on the beams that supported the roof. A layer of grass and weeds followed; then came a layer of earth. Finally the women would trample the earth with their feet. Houses shared walls and often were stacked on top of each other. One family's roof could be another family's front yard. Ovens could be built on the roofs, or skins could be laid out on the roofs to dry in the sun.

The stone and clay exteriors were well-suited to the hot climate. Because stone and clay soak up heat, the houses stayed cool during the day and warm at night. Doors and windows were kept small to keep out the heat of the blazing sun. Low doorways were wide at the top so that people with wide, heavy loads on their backs could fit through them. Until the Spaniards came, Pueblos didn't use stairways. In order to get into a home that was on an upper level, the Indians had to climb ladders, which could be pulled up in times of danger. This provided great protection from enemies who found it nearly impossible to enter the village.

Because their homes were small, the Pueblos had to be well-organized and neat. Ledges to be used as shelves were built into the walls. Special storage bins for grain and other foods were built into the floor. People did not use tables or chairs but sat on the floor or on top of rolled blankets. There were no beds either. The Indians slept on rugs or sheepskin.

It took a lot of work to maintain the home. Heavy rains often would wear down the clay plaster, making physical maintenance crucial. However, it was equally important to call upon the spirit world to preserve the home and protect its inhabitants. Important ceremonies were carried out during construction. Cornmeal was sprinkled on the floors to "feed" the house. The spiritual leader said prayers and hung special prayer feathers from the rafters to keep the house safe from harm. Then throughout the years, the prayer chief was called upon to renew the feathers.

Cliff Palace, Mesa Verde, Colorado, 1930.

Blue Lake, New Mexico.

The 20th Century

By the 20th century, the battle over Indian land and religion was no longer fought with weapons. Instead, political battles were waged. The Taos Pueblos' fight to preserve their sacred land remains one of the most pivotal Indian struggles to date. The fight gained the support of other Indian groups, as well as non-Indian Americans.

Under Mexican and American regimes, the Indians were often tricked into giving up their land. They didn't know that the American government would often break promises or make laws to suit its own interests. It wasn't long before Americans began pushing into Pueblo territory and settling on Pueblo land. The Taos were particularly concerned about Blue Lake and the area surrounding it. This land was within the boundaries of what the Indians believed the Creator had originally given the Pueblos' ancestors. The Pueblos often held sacred ceremonies at the lake. To the Indians, these ceremonies were necessary to maintain harmony in the natural world. By invading the territory, the whites threatened to disrupt the delicate balance that the Pueblo had worked so hard to preserve.

In 1903, President Theodore Roosevelt wanted to take Blue Lake and the surrounding shores and give it to the American people as a gift. He did not consider that it wasn't his to give. The Indians fought to make the area a reservation, but they lost. In 1908, 130,000 acres of sacred, Taos territory became part of Carson National Forest. American officials thought that the Native Americans could not be trusted to take care of the beautiful area. This was quite a shock and an insult to the Pueblos, who believed that it was their sacred mission to defend the earth. Ironically, they had managed to keep the lands pure for 600 years before the Americans decided to claim and protect the region from Pueblo tribes.

The Taos Indians complained that non-Indians trampled sacred sites, polluted rivers, and raised livestock without permission from the Indian settlers. At the same time, some American settlers fought bitterly to keep the Indians out of the Blue Lake territory. They even spread rumors that the Indians were conducting ritual murders! The Indians were conducting only peaceful, ceremonial rituals, but the settlers insisted that if the rites were secret, they must be evil. The Pueblos felt that they had to keep their rituals secret in order to protect themselves.

During the 1920s, different groups fought to banish Pueblo religious ceremonies entirely. The Indians fought for a chance to practice their ceremonies in private, without the intrusion of non-Indians, but it wasn't until the Indian Reorganization Act was passed in 1934 that the law protected the religion of Native Americans — at least on paper.

The Indian Reorganization Act proved to be just an empty promise. Even as late as 1965, government officials discouraged religious freedom on the grounds that the Pueblos would never understand the "civilized" way of life unless they were forced to give up their own culture. Different political organizations continued to fight for and against the Indians. At one point, the government offered to pay the Indians for Blue Lake, which the government had taken in 1908, but the Taos argued that their religion was more important than money.

The battle over the Blue Lake region came to symbolize the ongoing injusti-

ces to Native Americans. Non-Indians became angry, too. On behalf of the Taos, many supporters wrote letters to Congress as well as the President of the U.S., Richard Nixon. Nixon proved to be a friend of the Taos. Finally in 1970, after 62 years, the government returned 48,000 acres of land to the Taos tribe. This was an important victory for all Indians. At last, their rights to land and religious freedom were recognized by the American government.

(Photo courtesy of State Records and Archives, Santa Fe, New Mexico)

President Richard Nixon signs a bill returning 48,000 acres of land to the Taos people, December 15, 1970.

(Photos courtesy of
Museum of New Mexico)

*Left: Tom Toslino as he looked when he arrived at the
Carlisle School in Carlisle, Pennsylvania around 1880.
Right: Tom Toslino after three years at the Carlisle School.*

(Photo courtesy of State Records and Archives, Santa Fe, New Mexico)

Two Hopi kachinas.

Balancing Two Worlds

Today, Pueblo tribes have the difficult task of living in a modern society, while trying to preserve their ancient traditions. The challenge is to weave together two distinct ways of life.

Modern influences are evident on the reservations. Most Native Americans have abandoned the traditional sandstone houses for mobile homes or houses made of cement. Villages have been expanded beyond the original settlements, and most families live in houses with more than one room. A few families choose to live without modern conveniences. Some prefer to chop wood for fuel rather than use gas or electricity. The Pueblos still work on their own farms, but they use modern equipment. For economic reasons, some of the Native Americans have gotten jobs outside of the reservations.

Though their way of life is changing, the Pueblos keep focusing on spiritual

Cochiti Pueblo pupils at St. Catherine's School, Santa Fe, New Mexico.

values that are important to them. For example, the Hopis still believe that they are the guardians of the earth. Even today, they hold ceremonies for the protection of people, animals, plants, and minerals everywhere on earth.

Pueblo children were once forced to leave the reservation to attend school. In recent years, schools have been built on reservations, but the Bureau of Indian Affairs does not provide enough money for high quality education. In some schools, an entire class must share one book and sit on the floor because there are no chairs. In spite of such conditions, the Pueblos understand how important education is to their people. They know that if they are to succeed in the outside world and increase their standard of living, their young must be educated.

There has been much debate over whether Native American culture and language should be taught along with math and science. The Native Americans are particularly concerned about preserving their language. The Hopi language, for example, is in danger of becoming extinct because it has no written form. It must be spoken if it is to endure. Some Hopis are working to preserve their language through various mediums, including computers, videos, and recordings of traditional songs, poems, and oral histories.

The traditions that the Pueblos maintain are very important to them. A Hopi bridegroom is still given a wedding gift of cornmeal in a handmade basket. Though Pueblo teenagers wear modern hairstyles and sport tee-shirts with names of rock groups on them, many take time to learn tribal songs and hear their grandparents tell legends about their ancestors. Pueblo children understand that they are the future of their people. In a fast-paced and ever-changing world, the heavy burden of preserving their culture has been placed upon them.

Important Dates in Pueblo History

700 - 900	Pueblo culture first emerges.
1050 -1300	Pueblo culture reaches its peak.
1276 -1299	First major migration of Pueblo tribes takes place.
1450	Second wave of migrations takes place.
1540	Coronado arrives in the Southwest.
1598	New Mexico becomes a Spanish Colony.
1680	The Great Pueblo Revolt occurs.
1692	Spanish reconquer the Pueblos' territory.
1700's	Pueblos freed from Spanish tyranny.
1821	Mexico wins independence from Spain.
1848	Mexican-American War ends. The United States wins New Mexico.
1908	President Theodore Roosevelt makes the Blue Lake region part of Carson National Forest.
1920's	Pueblos fight for religious freedom.
1934	Indian Reorganization Act signed.
1970	President Richard Nixon returns Blue Lake area to the Taos.

INDEX